Following the Shepherd's Staff

Mary Annthipie Bane

DEDICATION

This book is dedicated to the ones who have lived the journey with me. To my family, my husband Terence and my sons Tyler, Cooper and Wesley. You are the loves of my life.

ACKNOWLEDGMENTS

Written with the acknowledgement of my Lord Jesus Christ and my Heavenly Father for only He could make something out of nothing.

INTRODUCTION

Portions of "Following the Shepherd's Staff"
were previously published under the title
"Confessions of a Church Hopper" and was
written for the edification of those who have
church traveled and for the understanding of
the seeking behavior. I am writing to
encourage and to lift up those who have
church traveled; some have traveled for
personal reasons and many have been
spiritually wounded; may you find the peace,
acceptance and healing that God alone can
provide. If you are one of the wounded I pray
for your emotional and spiritual healing. The
following is the story of my spiritual journey,
as it continues, while speaking His Word and
seeking Him first, following the Shepherd's
Staff all the while.

CHAPTER ONE

TRUE CONFESSIONS

This is the story of my personal confession. I am, apparently, so I've been told, a Church Hopper. Confession is good for the soul, and of course I believe that it is for God promised that this is true. We are instructed in 1 John 1:9, if we confess our sins, he is faithful and just to forgive us our sins, and to cleanse us from all unrighteousness. This is my confession by way of self-examination of a behavior that so many find confounding. I honestly didn't consider it a sin but if it has been offensive to my God than as according to His Word it needs to be addressed. "I acknowledge my sin unto thee, and mine iniquity have I not hid. I said, I will confess my transgressions unto the Lord; and thou forgavest the iniquity of my sin. Selah." Psalm 32:5.

It is also with this disclaimer that I write that in every church that I've participated in I have offered my service and utilized my spiritual gifts to the best of my ability and for a long as I have been able to do so. I haven't honestly considered that changing churches with the changing seasons of my life a sin, the name calling and judgmental words from others may possibly be.

I have not come to this place in my life where I am fully happy at home, marriage, motherhood and career without having traveled a bit. At times I have become travel weary. We are instructed to not become weary in doing good, but still I do have my moments of fatigue. I have traveled the circuit of the many and varied Christian denominations searching and seeking to expand my joy, knowledge and worship of the Lord. Some would call it church hopping, and have called it just that. To me it was following the Lord's leading, following the Shepherd's Staff where it should lead me, one of His sheep. This is the confession of a Church Hopper, uppercase, bold and italics, and confession is truly is good for the soul, along with prayer, praise, joy, hope, humility and understanding.

I am a wife, and a mother of three sons, an early childhood educator, a daughter, sister, aunt and friend. I am a born again Bible believing Christian. I am also, after much prayer, fasting and contemplation what I have only been able to describe with humor and love...and as I have been called...a Christian Gypsy, a traveler, a seeker. I have heard the phrase "church hopper" aimed in my direction, perhaps you have as well. I am at an age where many of you either have been or will find yourself, an age at which a becoming has taken place. Along with this process an opportunity to consider my ways has been provided.

My children are grown well into the teenage years, my marriage is blessed and my faith is unwavering. It has seen me through the joys of spiritual rebirth to the growing pains of Christian maturity and seasoning. I have become more fully myself in Christ Jesus and becoming all that He has created me to be. Endless prayer journals have been filled through the years, bible study workbooks have been devoured and Bibles of varying versions have been written in, highlighted, read, valued and treasured. It is with worn covers and tattered bindings that these Bibles sit on my shelf as a testimony to my love for His Word.

With the passing of the seasons of my life I have found that each not only has physical, emotional and financial needs which change, but each has spiritual needs that change also. Included in these changes has been an inner calling to seek and to, on occasion, move on. I have always understood "church" to be not only the denominational institution but in the greater sense, church for me is the body of believers. Romans 12:4-5 states, "For as we have many members in one body and all members have not the same office: So we, being many, are one body in Christ, and every one members one of another." The church is the collective group of sinners who are forgiven by grace and not of their own works. In Ephesians 2:8-9 we are told "For by grace are ye saved through faith; and that not of yourselves: it is the gift of God: Not of works, lest any man should boast." Not of works, not of deeds, not of church membership.

Church for me is and always will be the people for whom God so loved the world that he sent his only begotten son that whosoever believeth in Him should not perish but have everlasting life, John 3:16. This verse is well known is sporting arenas. Whether in the community church or worship center, in my personal life, in the workplace, the sporting arena or on the mission fields this is "church" to me.

Any church building and congregation have always been considered to be my home base of sorts, a room in the house of believers. Here we are to be instructed, strengthened, refreshed and renewed; offering our fellowship and service to one another so as to go out into the world and face our daily lives and the work God has set out before us to do. The home bases have changed for me over the years. In answer to those who have ventured to question, criticize or shun I simply reply: just because I've moved out of the house doesn't mean we aren't still family. Sadly there have been those Christian friends who have not held this same belief. I have been blessed however with an extended Christian family of believing sisters and brothers who through the expanse of change, time and distance have remained faithful non-judgmental friends in Christ.

The following writings are not intended to dissuade the regular, faithful and fulfilled church going member. That is a wonderful thing. There are some who have been raised in a church and are blessed to remain there. That has not been my story and I have come to discover that there are many more like me who have been led to seek and to search, to rest in the Lord and to reach out in fellowship and service once again. If you are like me and have had experience in Christian traveling then my hope is that the following pages will help you to feel less alone, at peace with your personal walk with God and in your relationship with Jesus Christ whose Word I have hidden in my heart. Thy word have I hid in mine heart, that

I might not sin against thee, Psalm 119:11. I have carefully reflected on my life a Christian Gypsy, a Journeyman of sorts, considering His ways better than my own and the lessons I have learned from every church I have visited and walked amongst.

In my most recent times someone had stated to me that if I have been in "x" number of churches in "x" number of years then perhaps it isn't the church at fault but something else, something inside of me. Of course it was something inside of me, that is where the journey of the soul take place; which believers know to be the temple of the Holy Spirit. It was a curious comment considering that I have never placed blame on any church. I have however always done my best to be open-minded and teachable.

When this statement was broached I began to reminisce, review and discover the purpose of my travels. My traveling ways, I believe, have been in accordance with God's will for my life and have been used to the edification of the body of believers in the sharing of the Gospel.

I have recently revisited the site of the churches of my youth. While I am certain that sending me off into yet another church was not the intended action my accuser had in mind it proved to be just the thing to bring my spirit life full circle. It appears that you can go home again and it has been a long, winding and wonderful road. I am home, not in "a" church but as a member of "the" Church.

In regards to what you are about to read, as a friend of mine and fellow writer is fond of saying "It isn't Shakespeare and it isn't intended to be." What exactly is intended by the journaling of a Church Hopping Christian Gypsy is to offer encouragement and share insights. It is not to offend or alienate anyone. In the simplest terms I intend the word Gypsy to imply -- traveler. It is an honest and sometimes light hearted look at a serious spiritual journey, one that I do not take for granted, but as it is written, a merry heart doeth good like a medicine. Proverbs 17:22.

CHAPTER TWO
SPIRITUALLY ADRIFT

I was not raised in what the born again community would consider an outwardly Christian home. My parents loved each other and their children. They were not regular churchgoers. Mom and Dad both felt disenfranchised from the religions of their youth: Roman Catholic and Greek Orthodox respectively, and were married in a beautiful and historic Episcopal church.

Signs of their faith were few in our home, my parents were not overtly spiritual, but signs of their faith did exist. An image of a Greek Orthodox Priest was a fixture on display set atop a miniature grandfather clock. Its artwork was similar to that of the Renaissance and I loved to look at it and gazed upon it frequently. There were a few crosses made of palms from Palm Sundays gone by. My mother had a religious medal on a chain; I believe it was the Miraculous Medal of the Virgin Mary.

We did not say grace at meals or have family devotions. There was a sense that a belief in God was present in the home but this was not typically verbalized. Being demonstrative in their feelings was not my parents' way, they were private people. I do not recall a family Bible but remember a small white pocket version of the New Testament with the words of Christ written in red. Those were the words I would turn to and read in my growing up years although I did not truly understand them. My parents were good people and my father worked hard to provide for his family. He was a strong personality and I believe that the good, healthy fear of his authority kept his children, for the most part, on the straight and narrow.

I can remember a plaque of the Twenty-Third Psalm with a beautiful image of Jesus, His shepherd's staff in one hand and a lamb gently cradled in His arms; a flock of sheep followed behind. I loved the imagery but did not understand the verse. "He maketh me to lie down in green pastures", and "the Lord is my shepherd I shall not want." As a child, of barely grade school age, I could not comprehend the beauty and grace of this loving, caring Savior. The verse must have had importance to be displayed in the home. The artwork and the words were so imprinted in my mind that I remember it to this day. They were also baffling to a spiritually adrift child. I wanted to learn more about this man named Jesus. I wanted to understand the green pasture and the meaning of a good shepherd and follow that shepherd's staff. These early events have in part fueled my interest in becoming an early childhood educator and have been the source of my desire for continuing biblical study. I write about the value and benefits of Christian Education in the early childhood years in my next book "Raised in His Ways".

I can also remember very clearly the day my mother realized that I did not know how to bless myself, as was her tradition when growing up as a practicing Catholic. At her reaction, surprise and sadness for this lack of most basic Christian instruction I felt shame and embarrassment. I was only of Kindergarten age and at this time my mother was beginning to struggle with the ravages of Rheumatoid Arthritis. This was a terribly painful and debilitating disease and she struggled with it for the rest of her life. The early stages of this illness were a partial reason for this lack of religious training. Sometime shortly afterwards she and I began to attend a neighborhood Episcopal Church and I fell in love with it.

I remember clearly the stained glass windows and was surprised to realize that my family history was there in that church. My mother's father had been the stonemason who had built the beautiful peanut stone fireplace. A memorial window pane with my late grandmother's name was displayed in the window of the last pew on the outer wall. This would be the pew my mother chose to sit in every Sunday. I never learned how someone from a Catholic background was memorialized in the Episcopal Church stained glass. My mother never volunteered that information and I never asked. Her loss was so great and it seemed too upsetting for her; the loss of her mother was heavy on her heart. It was something that even as a child I could understand. While sitting in that church pew it was the first time I can recall experiencing sympathy for someone. My first Christian values were being formed here; "Carry each other's burdens, and in this way you will fulfill the law of Christ."- Galatians 6:2.

I began to attend Sunday school and loved my teacher and new friends. I can clearly recall my classroom and classmates and still have an old, faded photograph. There I received a book of Children's Bible Stories which I still have today and have read to my own children. I learned the importance of Sunday worship where we remember Christ's sinless life, sacrificial death and glorious resurrection. My mother and I only attended for a brief time for about a year. She soon became too ill to visit regularly and we eventually stopped attending altogether.

That was my first hop into church life. It

wouldn't be my last and I carry those memories with me. They have been the first steps in shaping who I would become. It was a beautiful, sensory, spiritual experience. I remember church ladies in hats and children in their Sunday best. The lingering memories include beautiful sights, sounds, floral scents, candle light with flickering and elongated shadows, and most importantly feeling God's love for the first time. Jesus loves the little children.

During the time when my mother was laid up in bed she would entertain me with stories that she had created. Mom was a fabulous storyteller. My favorites were about two lively little bunnies ironically called "Hoppy and Jumpy". The thought of these stories still makes me smile. Just call me "Hoppy" but I fell in love with God at that age and with my random church attendance. I have been hopping along with Him ever since. It was the best gift my mom had ever given me, she introduced me to God, and she introduced me to a friend named Jesus. Growing up I would often stop and ask myself, "would God like this" and in my own spiritual yet immature way I had tried to allow Him to be my guide and I tried to be a good person. The lack of a continuing Christian education did lend itself to my drifting away from Him. There were times when I would question if he really were there. I feared that He wasn't but hoped that He was.

I would have occasion to visit that small church during the summers while growing up with my childhood friend and her family. They would invite me along and I gladly accepted the invitations. She remains a best friend today and we still remember these nearly forty years later about those times when I was their family hop along. It became my habit to visit churches whenever I was asked and able. Friends would invite for the morning after a slumber party church visit. I would accept. I loved weddings and christenings which provided more church visits to experience. There weren't many and I know that I can probably count them if I tried but I took great joy in my opportunity to visit God's house.

Through my growing up years I had visited the Episcopal, Baptist, Lutheran and Methodist Churches. They were all different from one another and yet they were all similar in that the people were welcoming and the Spirit of the Lord was present; a hopping I will go. Looking back now I suppose I have come by my hop-a-thon honestly and at an early age. It doesn't seem unusual or unchristian to me. I am still surprised at some of the superior and judgmental remarks, judge not please. Christian criticism abounds, unfortunately, and oh how easy it is to play the spiritual superiority game.

If you are out there reading this and are like me, pay no mind to the comments which are sometimes hurtful. Those who criticize know not what they do; they walk not in your church shoes. I know that when I wake up each morning with a praise song in my mind and a prayer of thanks on my lips, regardless of my circumstances, that it is well with my soul. If by church hopping gypsy name calling anyone intends to criticize my previous forty year long church habits, well, as I say to my prekindergarten class; "Worry about?" and all the children reply…."Yourself!" I shall follow the Lord as He leads.

Spiritually misguided you may be saying to yourself, immature, self-seeking. Yes I have been told those things in my adulthood, and many more comments like them than I care to share; judge not. Thankfully I live for Christ alone and not the approval of man or woman. What shall we then say to these things; "If God be for us, who can be against us", Romans 8:31. He walks with me and He talks with me and He tells me I am His own. His grace is sufficient for me and I will ever praise Him.

 In my youth I was spiritually adrift but had Jesus as my lighthouse and beacon, a lamp unto my feet, lighting the way to Him that I may follow that shepherd's staff. There was a time when I lost sight of God in my teen years. I dabbled in supernatural interests. Those curiosities lasted a few months and were squashed by a teacher who cared enough to take a prayerful action and set me back towards facing the light. I will be forever thankful for him. He was church to me, outside of the temple walls and in a high school classroom. My teacher, who was a Christian became the hands and words of God for me. I am reminded that we are the body whenever I think of him. We go about His work as parts of the body of Christ with Jesus as the head.

My childhood and teenage years moved along with my sporadic, eclectic church attendance. I was about to meet a young man who would change the course of my life. Interestingly enough we met on my eighteenth birthday, facing adulthood, leaving childhood behind, ready to leap.

CHAPTER THREE
LANDFALL

Landfall, Land Ho, the cry of the ancient mariners as they followed the North Star in the night sky and the shining lighthouse beacons as their guiding lights. Adrift no more they have arrived at their destination. Land is in sight, terra firma is near with its steadfast secure rock on which to stand until they journey forth again. As a lighthouse shines its light, thy Word is a lamp unto my feet, and a light unto my path, Psalm 119:105. Jesus is the rock of my salvation and I shall call on Him all the days of my life. It will be a life that involves seeking His will, listening for what was at one time that still small voice inside of myself and building upon a strong foundation, not built upon sand but upon the cornerstone who is Jesus.

After graduating from high school and during those last days before setting course for the world and destinations elsewhere I struggled with my purpose, with my plan. Long before any of us were so purposefully driven I sought after the reason why I was here. The question lingered in the air of the homeroom, locker room, school bus and around the cafeteria. It had been asked since those early days of kindergarten: what do you want to be when you grow up. What will you do with your life and if you're lucky enough to know, how then do you propose to make that happen. And the answer was, I have no idea.

Do what you love we are told, an artist, a teacher perhaps. I was not spiritually astute enough at the time to answer "Christian", I want to be a Christian. I want to be a follower of Jesus and not a follower of a denomination. If I look back now and I am honest with myself, that is the answer, everything else pales in comparison. I wish I had known the promise in Jeremiah 29:11, "For I know the thoughts that I think towards you, saith the Lord, thoughts of peace, and not of evil, to give you an expected end."

While just beginning my first few weeks of

college with pursuits in Fine Art I was introduced to a young man by a mutual friend. It was interest at first sight, which evolved into a friendship that grew into love and grows to this day. This is the man that I married six years and eight days after the first day we that we met.

To my surprise, after hitting it off I was asked out on a group date with our friends for the following Saturday. He would meet us after church. After church, did he say church? I hadn't been to a church or given church much thought in several years at that point let alone had I ever met a young man who willingly, voluntarily of his free will and accord, attended regularly every Saturday night. This was intriguing and placed him in a category all his own. I loved churches.

After many months of on again, off again dating we decided that on again suited us best. It was at this time that my first invitation to attend service together arrived. I happily agreed to accompany him. I was hesitant in that I didn't know what to expect. I was in awe. The size of the church was impressive, so unlike the small church of my childhood. The rows and rows of pews seemed to extend forever leading up to the altar which was breathtaking. I hopped right in. From organist to guitarist, to hymns, prayers and homilies I was hooked and became a regular attendee. Land Ho, I had landed. It took time for me to catch on to when we kneel, stand, sit, and when to recite, but I jumped at the chance to learn.

Having first fallen in love with Christian Education in Sunday school class as a child I was thrilled to continue as a young adult. Catechism classes were something that many of my friends attended while we were in school and seemed to be a mysterious thing of which I was not included. Now, once a week for several months I received instruction and a crash course of indoctrination into the Roman Catholic faith.

At the age of twenty-two I began my training in Catholicism. I marveled at the teachings of the sacraments, the lives of the Saints, church history and the stewardship of each member. With my young man who was now my fiancé as my "sponsor" I had finally found a church home and actually felt that I had in some way spiritually arrived at the place I had been seeking. I didn't know it was a stop on the journey, just a hop in the road. Soon we were attending Pre-Cana classes during our engagement and there we celebrated our wedding day. My time as a new member of the Catholic Church was a whirlwind of sacraments: communion, confirmation and a few months later, marriage. I chose the confirmation name "Faith", a fitting name agreed the priest and the bishop.

Five years after I had first been invited to church we were married, four years after that we were having our first child baptized and in three more years a second son was born. My time in the Catholic Church had been filled with activities, religion and faithfulness. I was however, beginning just before the birth of our first child, little by little being drawn away as a spiritual changeling. In the end I had spent twelve years attending the same church, which was a fair record for a church traveler like me. I felt that there was something coming next. The shepherd and His staff was calling.

CHAPTER FOUR
YE MUST BE BORN AGAIN

As they sing in the hymn, I verily, verily say
unto thee, ye must be born again. I had no idea
what that meant. I'd heard it before; thought it
was some radical group of folks left over from
the flower power generation that I had
observed as a child growing up in the
seventies. I certainly had never heard such talk
in my Catholic Church experience where I was
currently worshiping, it may have been
approached during the time of Confirmation,
but if it had been, at that time it didn't speak to
me.

The topic of sin, however, I had heard much
about and it intrigued me. During my time in
the Catholic Church I involved myself in
independent study regarding the lives of the
saints and researching the meaning of sin, the
mortal sins and the venial sins. I now
understand sin to be anything that you can
think, say, or do that God says in His word is

wrong. Sin separates us from God. It was a lot of information to keep track of, these major and minor sins and infractions. I would hear the words during each church service "Lord I am not worthy to receive you but only say the word and I shall be healed." Perhaps I was thinking too much about its meaning but the thoughts kept coming to me; what can anyone do to be worthy, what is the word I was waiting for God to say, and would I be healed. I assumed that "healed" meant from my sinful condition which seemed to be ever present.

It was 1993, the year before my first son was born and I was happily attending the church I was married in for several years. My paths had crossed with people who were "born again". I had heard this phrase before. When I was a teenager my aunt and uncle, my mother's sister and brother were members of a local church. I can remember the day one summer after attending a retreat they came to our home to share with my mom the good news that they were born again. Mom didn't understand it and neither did I. They gave me a Bible; I didn't know how to read it. I would look up topics in the index and hope to find insights there. I slept with it next to my bedside and during times of trouble, under my pillow.

When my aunt and uncle were born again they seemed to have something that I didn't have. I never talked with them about it and they never brought it up again for my mother was resistant to this idea. Looking back I realize that they had something in common with the born again people I was meeting. They had an inner peace that was elusive to me. They had a kind of joy that I hadn't yet known. They had a faith which gave them confidence that everything was going to work out just fine no matter what. They knew where they were going and I didn't. They had a friend in Jesus. Oh yes, I remember that from Sunday school but I hadn't given our friendship much thought for years.

I lit candles, said prayers to the saints and with my rosary, went to Novenas. I attended Mass which was still as beautiful, mystical and mysterious to me as it was the day I first attended. I was trying very hard to do those things that I thought were right. Still though, no peace, I had an unsettling begin to occur in my heart. A tugging was taking place and it was one more thing that I didn't understand.

Please don't misinterpret what I'm saying. I know that there are scores of practicing Catholics who have peace, love, joy, hope, faith and a relationship with God. At that time I just wasn't one of them, although I have come to be reconciled with these issues. I have friends and family who are practicing Catholics today and I love them all dearly. I have been drawn back there myself and I am in no way criticizing any church or church member. This has been the progression of my faith walk and not in any way, shape or form a reflection on anyone else. With that said and I hope it is understood with as much love as I can convey through my pen and keyboard, I write that I was seeking.

In those days my husband and I were involved in a network marketing business which frequently held meetings and business conferences. I had taken some business classes at our community college and worked in a hospital business office and I loved it. It was curious to me how many people we met at these networking sessions were "Christians". They did not identify themselves as Episcopal, Baptist, Lutheran, Methodist or any other denomination you can name. They identified themselves as Christians. I didn't understand that at all. I would ask what kind of Christian are you and they would answer "the Christian kind". Really, this was just another aspect of religious life that I just didn't understand. These conversations took place over coffee, in diners and living rooms, the meetings after the meetings, and they were fascinating.

I was a Christian, I celebrated Christmas and Easter. What on earth they were talking about I didn't know but my curiosity was sparked. These new friends and acquaintances of ours were nice, happy, interesting, centered and they had that inner quality, that peace, that knowing. My aunt and uncle had that. I didn't have those attributes but I admired them. I am reminded of the song, "this little light of mine, I'm gonna let it shine." I could see them shine their light and I was drawn to it. Again I add a disclaimer and please do not mistake me for saying that everyone who claims to be "born again" has these characteristics and by no means does "Christian" mean perfect person. This is simply what my experience had been, yours may be similar, or it may be different.

I had been seated in an enormous business seminar in the convention center in Atlanta, Georgia surrounded by several thousand people. Meeting new people and visiting new places was an exciting part of this business for me, it was fun and it was expanding upon the things I was learning in community college business classes. I do consider myself to be a lifelong learner. I suppose this is the reason that visiting new churches and meeting new people is equally fun for me.

At these business seminars it was thrilling to hear great motivational speakers. They brought a positive thinking message that I wasn't accustomed to but was thirsty for. Some people seem to come by that naturally but I wasn't one of them. I was more inclined to be pessimistic in nature. It was good for me to learn that I could change my mindset. It lifted the weight off my heart and was like breathing fresh air, but I needed to learn how, and I wanted to learn more.

One speaker in particular whom I will never forget, a woman from Australia, captured my full attention. She was bright, energetic, intelligent, successful, passionate about her topic and joyful. She spoke about relationships, how to genuinely build them, how to maintain and value them in our business and personal lives. She was vibrant, she was so full of so much honest and positive energy, she had a light, I'd seen that light before and I was drawn to it.

As she concluded her topic she took the time to share the details of the most important relationship in her life: the one she had with Jesus Christ. I was so surprised to hear the name of Jesus at a business seminar. He was here; he was outside the walls of the church. I was to come to learn that he was to be considered in all facets of life and not just remembered on Sunday, Christmas and Easter. She wasn't speaking of a generic higher power in the universe. She was speaking the name of Jesus, his sacrifice and his righteousness.

There it was, the plan of salvation, the manner in which we are able to change our ways, plainly and clearly laid out before me in the midst of literally thousands of people. She was speaking of being born again and she was speaking to me. I heard this message loud and clear just as surely and certainly as if we were the only two people in the room, in a diner, over coffee, chatting. For the first time I really heard the Gospel message. I not only hear it in my head but also in my heart. For the first time I had readily acknowledged that I was a sinner, not just a good person who sometimes sins. I was in need of a Savior and there is none other than Jesus. He is the way, the truth and the life, John 14:6.

It was a revelation to me that nothing I could ever do, say or become would grant me eternal life in heaven but that Christ alone died to take away the sins of the world, once, for all, so that our sins may be forgiven. "For whosoever shall call upon the name of the Lord shall be saved." Romans 10:13.

If there were only one person, if I or if you were the only one, He would have gone to the cross still, and thought of me, and you. Jesus was the sacrifice and He wants to have a relationship with me, and with you. He died for our sins, He rose again, and we'll live forever with Him. Jesus is the Word, the Word I was not worthy to receive but was given the free gift of His salvation through the cross. God's word that by his stripes I shall be healed; spiritually healed, emotionally, physically, eternally as it is written in Isaiah 53:5.

From that stage this speaker shared the plan of salvation, how to pray and that anyone may simply say that I know I am a sinner, thank Him for that free gift that He offered through His death on the cross, ask for forgiveness and invite Him into your heart for He is at the door waiting to come in. Upon hearing these words my face felt hot, my heart had a burning desire. As if a flame were upon my head a baptism in the Holy Spirit was taking place. I knew that God was speaking to me through her and it was time. I was finally to understand that the Lord is my Shepherd, that I had a Good Shepherd and He was calling me His own. For me it was a message both believed and received.

The next morning was Sunday and at a non-denominational worship service all who had received or would like to receive Jesus Christ as their Lord and Savior, their personal Savior, were asked to come forward and pray. I was up and out of my seat and didn't care who was watching or joining in. Jesus said to me "come" come unto Him and abide in Him, John 14:23. At the conclusion of the prayer for the hundreds who came forward in what I now know to be called an "altar call" the old nature was gone and a new creation had been born, 2 Corinthians 5:17. My spiritual birth had taken place and as it is written in John 3:7 "Marvel not that I said unto thee, ye must be born again". This was not a flower power expression; these are the words of Jesus. Thus saith the Lord, and I was born again.

We were all given a pocket sized New Testament; my mom had one of those, and an audio cassette which was titled "How to Study the Bible." Every one of us was encouraged to go home get a Bible in a version that we could understand and find a Bible based church in our area. I immediately purchased a Women's Devotional Bible and a notebook. Listening to the tape and immersing myself in personal Bible study was a step towards my next leap, my next hop along my spiritual journey.

CHAPTER FIVE
GROWING PAINS

Learning how to read my bible was liberating for me. No longer were the verses too profound to understand or the Bible just a dusty collection of ancient texts. I finally realized that I had access to the living Word of God, a veil had been lifted. This was the guidebook which for so long was locked to me, and suddenly I was given the key. I read, prayed and studied in my spare time, not wanting to waste another day without the knowledge of the scriptures.

Many people are fortunate to come to the spiritual place of being born again and have many friends and family members to mentor, disciple and share their new joy and faith. I had one co-worker and one family member who were born again to share my Christian walk with. My husband did not share my enthusiasm at that time although he does today and I'm thankful for that. In my born again infancy stage I was on my own with an audio cassette by a powerfully motivating, nationally known Christian speaker who years later I would have the privilege to briefly meet again and to share my joy.

I popped in my cassette and turned to the book of John, taking notes and pausing to write and reflect. I learned that "In the beginning was the Word, and the Word was with God, and the Word was God. The same was in the beginning with God" John 1:1-2. I turned to Genesis 1:26 and learned that the text reads; "let us make man in our image", the Trinity was there in the beginning. I celebrated my new beginning with the spiritual milk of God's love. I moved on to learn the Beatitudes with the moving and thought provoking Sermon on the Mount in Matthew 5:3-12. I poured over "The Love Chapter" in 1 Corinthians 13 and "The Faith Chapter" in Hebrews 11. I embraced the reading of the Psalms and Proverbs. I learned that love is not merely a feeling or a greeting card sentimentality but love is a decision, love is action, God is love, 1 John 4:16.

God's agape love for us was so great and so vast that Jesus stretched His arms out wide to demonstrate His love on the cross. The reality of that act was becoming more meaningful to me. That was not a myth; it was not a fairy tale story. There was a record of Jesus' birth, his life and his death. There was an eyewitness account to His resurrection and ascension into heaven. This was real. This was for me. With this new found faith and knowledge I would ponder in my mind and heart, what would I do with it and how would I live my life, for me, that was the question.

To develop a Christian character and respond to people, places and events as Jesus did would take time, practice and effort. It was not an overnight transformation. I learned that my faith must be exercised; this exercise is provided by walking with God. These would be baby steps with growing pains along the way, missteps and mistakes. I continued studying God's Word with the help of a Christian talk radio station, my bible study

cassette and the devotions that we an addition
in my bible. I was soon listening to biblical
instructions and reading Christian educational
books and magazines whenever possible. This
was before the days of a computer and internet
access in every home. I would go to the public
library and a local Christian bookstore. This
went on for a little over a year. My first born
came along and I became a stay at home mom.
Our son had severe medical challenges as the
result of an extreme bilirubin level. My new
faith saw me through that time, it was
heartbreaking but God is faithful and He used
it to build my Christian maturity and my trust
in Him.

All the while during this early bible study and
becoming a mother I was still attending the
church we were married in. I took seriously
instructions in 1 Timothy 2:15 to study to
show thyself approved unto God. While
attending our Catholic Mass I would compare
my studies and Christian walk with my church
life, there were things that I couldn't seem to
reconcile with; back then, the two didn't seem

to match up for me. I felt like I was living a double life with the Holy Bible as my personal authority and church tradition dictating my worship. I can now attend Mass without these conflicting thoughts and feelings, but back then it was a part of my spiritual growth and journey. As I look around the church on my visits today, I see Jesus, hear His Gospel preached and sit among His people who strive to live their faith in Him every day.

After the birth of my second child and having him christened I began to slow down in my church attendance until it had stopped completely. Eventually I would begin to tune into televised church services and I prayed for an answer.

I was being called to move in a new direction, not away from something but towards something else. It wasn't an easy thing and I didn't take that decision lightly. It was painful and it was through the fault of no one. I was being stretched in my faith and being called to move, to hop along, and so, I did.

I had begun to inquire about homeschooling my children and as was my habit I did my research at the local public library. I found a homeschool group that met in a Baptist church not far from my home. I had often driven past on a Sunday morning and wondered what it was like in there. Seeing the families and all of the children caused me to long to be a part of it.

I had somehow received a free trial issue of a Christian magazine. At this stage I was a stay at home mom with two children, a three year old and a baby. I had no other friends nearby who had children or who were churchgoers. I anxiously waited for my free issue hoping to read parenting and support articles. When it came I opened it up to a double page article featuring a mothers association. I had never heard of such a thing and excitedly called the toll free number to find a group near me. As it turned out there was a group that met in the Baptist homeschool group church. It was the church I had always wanted to visit. I was ready to hop in with both feet and I did.

My first visit caused me to join the homeschool and mothers groups. I was making new friends, feeling like I belonged and not alone or lonely in my Christian faith. I made friends that I still have to this very day. After a few months of this group participation, in November of 1998 our family attended services there together and we never looked back. Shortly afterwards I discovered I was expecting our third child. It was an enormous leap of faith and fellowship, one that I'm still so happy to have made. It was a step along on my journey, in my spiritual life and education. This was my walk thus far with Jesus by my side.

For five years we not only attended but participated in every manner of worship, service and get-togethers. My husband and I were baptized in a full water immersion baptism. Our three children were dedicated to the Lord there. I grew to know nearly everyone and they grew to know our family. I was moved to participate in Christian service and I loved it. By now my baby steps had developed into growing pains. My family life was changing. September 11, 2001 had played a role in our family life but we were intact. There were days when I feared that I would be swept away by confusion and emotional distress but I kept my eyes on God. I clung to the verse in Psalm 121:2 "My help cometh from the Lord, which made heaven and earth". With help like that I knew I would be alright. My feet were planted on the rock of Jesus, I held onto him through the storm.

Much had taken place in my personal life in those five years that we attended this church. During this time our third child was born, my parents had both been very ill and had died within two years of each other. We were heartbroken that our country was now at war. I developed some personal medical issues. My Christian service was becoming less joyful and more burdensome, I didn't want it to be but it was. I was homeschooling our young children. I was burned out. I was fractured. I felt broken. I needed a rest and I hopped out. Through the fault of no one, my time there came to an end. I had developed from a new Christian on spiritual milk to one who was now being fed on spiritual solid food. The good news is that growing pains don't last and neither do storms, they both come in order to pass. I hopped along. Five years wasn't too bad for a church hopper like me.

"I love the Lord, because He hath heard my voice and my supplications. Because He hath inclined His ear unto me, therefore I will call upon Him as long as I live." Psalm 116:1-2. So too that it was that I loved church attendance; the people, the prayers, the praises, and soon began attending a pretty little Baptist church in our neighborhood. It fit the bill perfectly. There were some homeschoolers there and some very dear friends and I was able to renew myself and gain my spiritual strength.

By this time church for me had become an institution of higher learning on a biblical level as well as a house of worship. I was also learning that even in the Protestant churches of like denomination there were varying doctrinal schools of thought and we tried to find one that fit. I wanted that joy that I had felt from my first church experience and also my born again renewal. I needed a spiritual revival and so a-visiting we did go.

Forgive me please my reader if this offends but it isn't intended to. If only it would be as the Bible proclaims that we may be perfectly joined together as it is written in 1 Corinthians 1:10. I would like to say that we had found a home during those growing pains years but rather we had found temporary shelters in which we were to love and serve.

At one point in more recent years I had been hired as church staff where my duties were in administration and dealt with assisting in worship. I was thrilled to work in a church, grew to love the people and learned about the Presbyterian ways which are beautiful and orderly. I found great satisfaction in my humble part time position, it is what I had studied for and was trained to do and I loved it.

This work tended to conflict with my personal

church attendance and I felt that if a choice were to be made between the two I just couldn't do it. Jesus loved them both, and I did also. The weight of trying to be all things in two separate places soon caused me to grow weary. Apparently my spiritual stamina and my physical stamina had yet to be calibrated. I had been working with the youth in Sunday school and at the school year's end I then concluded my service in the Baptist Church we had been attending.

While working at the Presbyterian Church I would attend there and was available on Sunday mornings should they have a need for me. I hopped out of the third Baptist Church, not out of intention but out of what seemed to be necessary.

Church work and teaching have always been my love, my hope, my dream and I followed it. For those of you who may be like me, I hope I am clear that I do not and never did "church hopping" out of spite or malice. I never considered it a dirty word or a criminal offense. I am not writing to encourage people to take up their religious roots and run around collecting church bulletins. It does seem to me that Jesus travelled, Peter and Paul travelled too. The apostles and today's missionaries all travel. Catholic priests travel from diocese to diocese. I have travelled, which is not to be confused with wandering. I have a destination. I am running the race with patience that God has set before me Hebrews 12:1.

My part time work came to an end due to economic changing times. I was called to accept a full time teaching position of prekindergarten aged children. This early childhood education work, next to my marriage and children, who are my first priority, love and ministry, is a joy. I was now not attending any church and was a homebound Christian waiting on the Lord to move me, and move me He did in His perfect timing.

One Easter Sunday our family attended the church of my childhood which is now a non-denominational Christian Church. It is a full circle moment that I have hopped into. I visit on Sundays and gaze upon that same peanut stone fireplace which I had admired as a child. During the service I listen to the dynamic and spirit filled message and cannot help but to "turn my eyes to the hills" and take in the beauty of this pretty little chapel.

I sometimes sit in the pew that I sat in as a child. The names of the dearly departed have been replaced with the names of the Fruit of the Spirit; love, joy, peace, patience, kindness, goodness, faithfulness, gentleness and self-control. It is fitting that this is all I seek, this is all I ask and all that I hope to offer. The verse in Galatians 5:22-23 is painted over a doorway in my home. The Fruit of the Spirit is the result of the indwelling of the Holy Spirit, my lifelong love of God, and relationship with His Son. If I had not hopped to it, I would have missed it all.

CHAPTER SIX
SERVICE AS UNTO THE LORD

I want to share with everyone how very important I believe it is to serve God and His people, those who call themselves Christian and those who do not yet have a relationship with Him. The very best gifts are gifts from the heart and God loves a cheerful giver, 2 Corinthians 9:7. Let nothing be done through strife or vainglory; but in lowliness of mind let each esteem others better than themselves. Philippians 2:3.

If you are a steadfast church attendee, a traveling church hopper or an at home Christian, Christ has given us the example of how to be of service. We are to love one another, John 13:34. How frequently do we find those who complain, they are there to condemn and criticize. If Christians and churches understood the action of love, how many more people would be drawn to the Savior. God loves us with an everlasting love and underneath are the everlasting arms. We are to be the love of Jesus to all people, created in His image which in itself is love.

I have researched extensively and have had discussions with church hoppers in person and on blogs across the internet about the need for service. If we call ourselves "Christian" then we understand that name to mean "Little Christ", Christ-like. Jesus was the Master Teacher and showed us the way to love one another; not in word alone but also in deed. Jesus fed the thousands, Jesus washed the feet of the disciples, and Jesus prayed and was a kind and loving friend.

The power of the Holy Spirit dwells in each believer, for we are the temple of the Holy Spirit and thus are endowed with certain Spiritual gifts. We are not all called to be pastors or preachers. Consider the things and activities which you feel passionate about, and also those things that you are naturally talented in. Think about these things as you seek to participate. No act of service is too small or unimportant or to be compared with the works of anyone else.

If you are visiting a church and there is a coffee fellowship ask those who have coordinated if there is a way you can be of help to them. It may be as simple as holding a door open for someone. If you are a regular visitor greet people as they arrive, introduce yourself, wish them a pleasant day. For some of our senior citizens and elderly you may be one of the few people that they will see for the rest of the day. We are to look for opportunities to be kind. Chat with a new or expectant mother about their baby and offer a word of encouragement.

If you are a regular attendee, look for areas that your gifts can be of use to the membership and community. It may be tidying up the pews and picking up left behind bulletins. Check your church mission board and write letters or regularly pray for the missionaries. Remember the church prayer list and lift them up to the Lord during the week. There are ample ways to serve the church or churches that you or I hop in and around.

Regular church membership has Christian service opportunities to utilize everyone's spiritual gifts and time allowances. Children's ministries, Sunday school, bible study, donating to the food pantry and ushering are just a few of the areas in which to participate. Ask your pastor or check your church bulletin or newsletter. Larger churches will have committees, smaller ones may have a team of just a few but faithful leaders. In whatever situation I have found myself having hopped in to I have offered my time and service. It is a joy to be in the house of the Lord. Serving God's people is the most rewarding aspect of settling into a church as a member for me. Helping out as a visitor makes the visits worthwhile.

My first ministry is and always will be to my family. When their needs are provided for I am more than happy to hop right in. Should our family life and circumstance be altered in some way, my service outside of the home is scaled back accordingly until such time that it can be resumed. The blessing of being a part of the body of Christ is that another member is there to offer their services should any one part find themselves no longer able to function. In whatever the area of service you or I choose, as a hopper, do so as unto the Lord. You will bless those around you and will be blessed in return. Hop as unto the Lord in a manner that will bring Him all of the honor and glory. It is a means in which we may show Him our love.

CHAPTER SEVEN
CONSIDER YOUR WAYS

Do not forsake the assembling of ourselves together, Hebrews 10:25. There are Christians who regularly attend services, those who habitually visit different churches from week to week, those who stay for a time and move on and those who stay home. There is no one right way to be a follower of Jesus Christ. Love Him with all of your heart, soul, mind and strength for this is the greatest commandment. We are also taught that the second is like it and we are to love our neighbors as ourselves, Mark 12:31.

There are Christians who lead large church ministries, those who worship in small home groups and those who view televised services. All are capable of fully walking with the Lord. Judge not. Church attendance is not an admission ticket into heaven. There are also those dear brothers and sisters in Christ who have been spiritually wounded by "the church". Spiritual abuse comes in many shapes and forms from the blatant to the subtle. I prefer to discern by prayer and watchful attention for signs of any abuse of power.

I have invested my time and energy in the study of spiritual abuse through online support groups to help myself understand and empathize with the consequences. I will not be writing about the physical abuse that has taken place in churches. This is a grievous act to our God and against our fellow humans.

I will be addressing the subtle signs of spiritual abuse, but I must implore you, if you are being physically abused by anyone -- do not hop, run and contact your law enforcement. Let no one purposefully harm you and then tell you to turn the other cheek. This has not been my experience but we know it exists; it is a sinful, crying shame which disgusts me. Do not be deceived, do not be manipulated, do not allow yourself to be in harm's way, if you find yourself there, run.

Much more common and generally unspoken

are the manipulators, the connivers, the charlatans, the operators, the controllers. I have talked to and prayed with individuals and families who have been exposed to this kind of spiritual abuse more often than I truly care to think about.

We see in the news the so called churches that charm snakes, taint beverages, or plan to meet on a spaceship. Clearly don't hop -- run! I am not addressing this behavior. To me there is another destructive and sinister abuse which causes one to question their faith and their walk with God; that would be the activity of the slick and the shady. They come in humble ways as a wolf in sheep's clothing. Their ultimate goal is control. They want to have you or I believe that we need them, that we belong to them, that they are owed something by you and by me. Make not for yourself any false gods including worship of a pastor, preacher or teacher.

I have been blessed to know fine, knowledgeable, caring and kind pastors, preachers and teachers who emulate Christ's love in their lives. I am in no way, shape or form implying to beware of every church. We should however be as wise as serpents and as harmless as doves, Matthew 10:16. The good pastor speaks God's Word, His truth in love, not for his or her own benefit but for the benefit of God's people, for the furtherance of His Kingdom.

A price was paid for you; the precious blood of Jesus has redeemed us from our sins. He has come to set us free and not to place us in bondage to spiritual abuse. The words of a hymn play in the background of my life; "Now I belong to Jesus, Jesus belongs to me, not for the sake of time alone, but for eternity." Not for church attendance, not for church membership, not for the approval of others, but for an eternity with Him.

It is my personal, heartfelt desire to participate in worship that is steeped in God's Word and praises Father, Son and Holy Spirit. As a busy family with three active teenaged sons, we have had our weekly scheduling challenges. I have learned to keep the Sabbath Holy by remembering Him, His life, His sacrifice, His love.

I would ask that you please not judge the church hopper. I have found online information claiming that we are everything from users to church bulletin collectors. I will not and do not go round and round the mulberry bush of church visitations for fear of making a commitment or for fear of building relationships. It matters not to me if the church I visit offers the best coffee or an after service brunch. These are not the reasons that I attended various church services. I am not out to see what I can get.

"Gypsy" you may still be thinking to yourself; Christian Gypsy I have been told. Be very careful so as not to end up with a beam in your eye, Matthew 7:3. I am also not writing to encourage reckless and foolish behavior. Be very careful not to go from church to church to tear the body apart.

I have learned from the many people I have talked to and prayed with over the years. I have learned that there are those who are hoppers and those who are hoppees. The hoppees are those usually well-meaning Christians who may potentially frighten off the hopper like a timid rabbit. Typically hoppers do not care to be judged, scrutinized, followed and imposed upon. I have not hopped along due to an unwillingness to commit myself to God; some hoppers will hop along for that very reason and that's their right to do so. Some hoppers hop along because they are fearful, lost or hurt. We need to be sensitive to their needs.

If the hopper doesn't make an appearance in the church for a few weeks it is sometimes because they like to step back and evaluate. Trust that they know the location of the church; it's usually the building with the bell and the cross. They remember how to get there and what time service is. A hopper is first a decision maker and an internal debater before they make the move to hop. If they need time to themselves it is usually in everyone's best interests to respect their boundaries.

Sometimes well-meaning efforts to reach out to the hopper is interpreted as pushy, overbearing, or controlling, all of the things which the hopper may be trying to avoid. The true hopper doesn't typically want anyone showing up at their door unannounced or uninvited. They want their preferences respected, they often have suffered from control issues in their life, and they don't want church to be one more. The little sparrow, which God has His eye on, hops along looking for crumbs. If you run at it screaming and shouting that you have what it needs it will fly away. Some hoppers are like that. Just go along doing the Lord's work and let them be. If they do not feel threatened, they will return.

I have spoken to hoppers who appreciate the church who conducts itself in the same manner whether two, twenty-two or two thousand-two people are in attendance. God's truths must be taught through the sermon but churches preach the Word, don't get caught up in trying to control the members and allow

God to do the work. A church must be managed; its time, material resources and its spiritual resources need to be used effectively. It is beneficial to the membership if the church knows its purpose and conducts itself accordingly. I've known many hoppers who wished that the church would focus on its mission and simply accept the people who attend where they are at and allow them to come as they are.

Spiritual maturing cannot be forced, cajoled or manipulated, it comes in time and it comes in God's time. We are to preach the Word and share the Good News which is the Gospel of Jesus Christ while we love one another. When we plant the seeds and tend to the needs we will witness the arrival of the bountiful harvest.

A word to the hoppees, hoppers do not typically like other folks in their personal business. They will take offense if their Sunday youth athletic leagues, dance recitals or work is being criticized. Share the scriptures regarding these teachings but rest assured that they know the Word of God on the matter and let them be and let God work within them. This is a part of their spiritual journey that they must go through. Hoppers will not want to be told to ignore visiting family members and have the church insist they bring them to service. Hoppers want their boundaries respected and if they sense that they aren't, they may just put on their hopping shoes. I've spoken to many hoppers and there seems to be a recurring theme that they didn't feel respected, they felt put upon and uncomfortable, even if it may or may not have deliberately been the case. If a correction or a suggestion needs to be made, do so gently and in love so that the hearer may receive the message.

We live in a society of emotionally battered and weather weary people; respect their boundaries, respect their time. In the long run they will become strong, mature, loving Christians if they are granted the proper time for growth. I've known unbelievers who were more respectful of personal boundaries and needs. This should never be.

We are to offer respect to others as Christ

offered Himself on the cross. We must remember to consider others better than ourselves. If a hopper tells us that they are busy or feeling unwell they do not want scripture reminders sent to them. Here's another hopping confession, that's usually just their excuse. Let them be, pray for them and let God do the convicting, and He will. We should of course preach the truth of God's Word in love but let us not hit anyone over the head with it.

In my travels and in my studies I have found hoppers to come from all different backgrounds and walks of life. Some are conservative, shy or insecure so please don't ask them to be more demonstrative in service than they are comfortable with. If it is God's will their interaction will develop as their feeling of spiritual security within the church walls develops. If they feel awkward, they will hop away, and that's a shame. For a lack of respect a potential regular church goer hops away.

I once heard someone say after witnessing a

"mature Christian" argue and completely disrespect someone; this is the reason I will never join a church she told me, they think they own you. This should never be and that is so sad. Don't impose yourself on anyone, hoppees and hoppers alike. Jesus drew them in with love and they followed Him. He told stories in the form of parables and gave them things to think about in order to help them grow. These are the things I have learned about hoppers and hoppees and about myself.

Hoppees, do not exasperate the hopper. Please never play the holier than thou game. Here's another confession, hoppers don't like it. Hoppers, don't be so easily offended, the hoppees usually mean well but sometimes, like everyone, they will make mistakes, say things they didn't mean or unknowingly hurt someone's feelings. Hoppers, extend the grace to them that you would like to have extended to you, don't look for reasons to hop, if you do, you are sure to find them. Look for reasons to stay and worship and grow in the wisdom and knowledge of the Lord.

Hoppers remember, don't be abused, but don't be overly sensitive and immature either. Hoppers, if you find you have a tendency to be spiritually needy please respect the church, attend services and consider the teachings there. Give yourself time to grow and become a part of the body of the believers where you are. So often we can all wear each other out.

There is no perfect person, there is no perfect church and if you look for it, you will surely be disappointed. As it is written, there is none righteous, no not one, Romans 3:10. There are however those who have a heart for God, and there are His people who desire to be like Jesus, yoke yourself with those. Christianity is a wonderful all you can eat buffet of churches, teaching, preaching, worship styles and doctrines, if you have sampled them, don't overindulge yourself, pick one; taste and see that the Lord is good. Hopping for too long can cause spiritual motion sickness, don't let that happen.

I would encourage you and encourage myself to not seek to fill a void by moving from church to church but rather to cast your cares on Him. He is the Great Physician, the healer of all our hurts. God alone is the provider of all our needs. If anyone must hop try to do so in a way that will keep you hopping towards our Heavenly Father and may we jump into His eternal and everlasting love for us. Be transformed by the renewing of your mind and not your location. It is not easier said nor easier done but it is possible; for all things are possible with God. Speaking His word and remaining in His perfect will is needed and necessary in order to live the abundant life He created us to live.

This is my story. It is a relatively short story of my lifelong spiritual journey. It may be similar to yours, it may not be, I hope that above all things it is the work that He has set out for me to do as I follow the shepherd's staff. We are here to do the work of God and the work of God is this; that ye believe on Him whom He hath sent, John 6:29. That is what I have set out to accomplish. Love the Lord your God in the manner and time and place that you see fit and when we mature it's time to settle down, find a home and put down some spiritual roots. My traveling salvation show has come to rest in the place where it began and so my story will continue there. I have "come right round."

I have also learned this, sometimes we are the hopper but we can easily become the hoppee. Our words matter, our words are powerful, make them God's words and build each other up. Remember always to love one another and love those who come into your life, and those who move on. People will visit churches, some will stay and some will go and some will visit again. Love them as Jesus does; for at the end of the church service, at the end of the day, the kingdom and the power and the glory are God's across the denominations, now and forever.

Following the Lord's leading has been and continues to be the yearning of my heart. Church traveling, seeking the shepherd and his staff, has been my path.

In my adulthood: church number one taught me the differences between tradition and biblical truth, how they work together and of the wonder working power of Christ's blood.

Church number two taught me about redemption, salvation, bible study and fellowship, a love for praise music, teaching and using your spiritual gifts in the service of others to God's glory.

Church number three taught me the love of traditional Hymns, and a love for the King James Version of the Bible, however I do still value my NIV, Amplified and American Standard.

Church number four taught me the value of an education steeped in theology and inadvertently led me to pursue my seminary degree.

Church number five solidified my heartfelt belief in the power of God's Word in our daily lives.

A sixth church which made appearances in my

life in between the others taught me about the Holy Spirit and living the spirit filled life. It provided renewal, rest in the Lord and a home away from home.

And throughout this time I not only gleaned, but offered: hands and a heart for service, teaching, care and instruction of God's children, directing Women's Bible Studies, hospitality, encouragement, ministry leadership, a voice in the choir, and dedication as a faithful prayer warrior. The staff of Jesus led me both inside and outside the walls of the church building. It led me in the service of the saved as well as for the lost and the seeking. The staff of Christ is my guide, my constant and is very nearly as symbolic of my faith as is the cross. The staff reassures me that I belong to Him and that while churches and church memberships may come and go, I shall never be departed from my shepherd, my Savior.

``I am often asked, what church are you going to now? What church do you belong to? To both of these questions which are sadly often meant to judge and not just to inquire, no matter however, I reply to those with Christ's love: I do not belong to "A" church, I belong to "THE" Church, the full body of believers which dances across the denominations. I encourage Christians within and across the denominations to "be" the Church.

Once again I light candles, say prayers not "to the saints" but as if they were dear friends whom I am asking to pray for me. I often also pray the Rosary, the very same which so many Christians have prayed before us, not for the worship of Mary but to contemplate the life of Christ through the eyes of his mother and as it is written in John 19:27, "and to the disciple, "Here is your mother." From that time on, this disciple took her into his home." I have welcomed her into my home. The saints and Mary, Christians whose lives were the epitome of the Christian faith and the Christian walk, whose lives teach us to follow the shepherd's staff, not for their own worship but for that of Jesus Christ, examples for us all, if you so choose. I attend Mass which is still as beautiful, mystical and mysterious to me as it was the day I first attended. May we all to look for the guidance of the staff, belonging to the Shepherd; whose sacrifice has redeemed his flock, that we shall eternal life with Him.

Matthew 5:1-12
New International Version (NIV)

Introduction to the Sermon on the Mount

Now when Jesus saw the crowds, he went up on a mountainside and sat down. His disciples came to him, [2] and he began to teach them.

The Beatitudes

He said:

[3] "Blessed are the poor in spirit,
　　for theirs is the kingdom of heaven.
[4] Blessed are those who mourn,
　　for they will be comforted.
[5] Blessed are the meek,
　　for they will inherit the earth.
[6] Blessed are those who hunger and thirst for righteousness,
　　for they will be filled.
[7] Blessed are the merciful,
　　for they will be shown mercy.
[8] Blessed are the pure in heart,
　　for they will see God.
[9] Blessed are the peacemakers,
　　for they will be called children of God.
[10] Blessed are those who are persecuted

because of righteousness,
    for theirs is the kingdom of heaven.

[11] "Blessed are you when people insult
you, persecute you and falsely say all kinds of
evil against you because of me. [12] Rejoice and
be glad, because great is your reward in
heaven, for in the same way they persecuted
the prophets who were before you.

Psalm 23

The Lord is my shepherd; I shall not want.

² He maketh me to lie down in green pastures: he leadeth me beside the still waters.

³ He restoreth my soul: he leadeth me in the paths of righteousness for his name's sake.

⁴ Yea, though I walk through the valley of the shadow of death, I will fear no evil: for thou art with me; thy rod and thy staff they comfort me.

⁵ Thou preparest a table before me in the presence of mine enemies: thou anointest my head with oil; my cup runneth over.

⁶ Surely goodness and mercy shall follow me all the days of my life: and I will dwell in the house of the Lord for ever.

1 Corinthians 13

The Love Chapter - NIV

If I speak in the tongues of men and of angels, but have not love, I am only a resounding gong or a clanging cymbal. ² If I have the gift of prophecy and can fathom all mysteries and all knowledge, and if I have a faith that can move mountains, but have not love, I am nothing. ³ If I give all I possess to the poor and surrender my body to the flames,ᴵ but have not love, I gain nothing.

⁴ Love is patient, love is kind. It does not envy, it does not boast, it is not proud. ⁵ It is not rude, it is not self-seeking, it is not easily angered, it keeps no record of wrongs. ⁶ Love does not delight in evil but rejoices with the truth. ⁷ It always protects, always trusts, always hopes, always perseveres.

⁸ Love never fails. But where there are prophecies, they will cease; where there are tongues, they will be stilled; where there is

knowledge, it will pass away. [9] For we know in part and we prophesy in part, [10] but when perfection comes, the imperfect disappears. [11] When I was a child, I talked like a child, I thought like a child, I reasoned like a child. When I became a man, I put childish ways behind me. [12] Now we see but a poor reflection as in a mirror; then we shall see face to face. Now I know in part; then I shall know fully, even as I am fully known.

[13] And now these three remain: faith, hope and love. But the greatest of these is love.

Hebrews 11 - The Faith Chapter NIV

Now faith is being sure of what we hope
for and certain of what we do not see. [2] This is
what the ancients were commended for.

[3] By faith we understand that the universe was
formed at God's command, so that what is
seen was not made out of what was visible.

[4] By faith Abel offered God a better sacrifice
than Cain did. By faith he was commended as
a righteous man, when God spoke well of his
offerings. And by faith he still speaks, even
though he is dead.

[5] By faith Enoch was taken from this life, so
that he did not experience death; he could not
be found, because God had taken him
away. For before he was taken, he was
commended as one who pleased God. [6] And
without faith it is impossible to please God,
because anyone who comes to him must
believe that he exists and that he rewards those

who earnestly seek him.

7 By faith Noah, when warned about things not yet seen, in holy fear built an ark to save his family. By his faith he condemned the world and became heir of the righteousness that comes by faith.

8 By faith Abraham, when called to go to a place he would later receive as his inheritance, obeyed and went, even though he did not know where he was going. 9 By faith he made his home in the promised land like a stranger in a foreign country; he lived in tents, as did Isaac and Jacob, who were heirs with him of the same promise. 10 For he was looking forward to the city with foundations, whose architect and builder is God.

11 By faith Abraham, even though he was past age—and Sarah herself was barren—was enabled to become a fatherbecause he[a] considered him faithful who had made the promise. 12 And so from this one man, and he as good as dead, came descendants as

numerous as the stars in the sky and as countless as the sand on the seashore.

13 All these people were still living by faith when they died. They did not receive the things promised; they only saw them and welcomed them from a distance. And they admitted that they were aliens and strangers on earth. 14 People who say such things show that they are looking for a country of their own. 15 If they had been thinking of the country they had left, they would have had opportunity to return. 16 Instead, they were longing for a better country—a heavenly one. Therefore God is not ashamed to be called their God, for he has prepared a city for them.

17 By faith Abraham, when God tested him, offered Isaac as a sacrifice. He who had received the promises was about to sacrifice his one and only son, 18 even though God had said to him, "It is through Isaac that your offspring will be reckoned." 19 Abraham reasoned that God could raise the dead, and figuratively speaking, he did receive Isaac back

from death.

[20] By faith Isaac blessed Jacob and Esau in regard to their future.

[21] By faith Jacob, when he was dying, blessed each of Joseph's sons, and worshiped as he leaned on the top of his staff.

[22] By faith Joseph, when his end was near, spoke about the exodus of the Israelites from Egypt and gave instructions about his bones.

[23] By faith Moses' parents hid him for three months after he was born, because they saw he was no ordinary child, and they were not afraid of the king's edict.

[24] By faith Moses, when he had grown up, refused to be known as the son of Pharaoh's daughter. [25] He chose to be mistreated along with the people of God rather than to enjoy the pleasures of sin for a short time. [26] He regarded disgrace for the sake of Christ as of greater value than the treasures of Egypt, because he was looking ahead to his reward. [27] By faith he left Egypt, not fearing

the king's anger; he persevered because he saw him who is invisible. ²⁸ By faith he kept the Passover and the sprinkling of blood, so that the destroyer of the firstborn would not touch the firstborn of Israel.

²⁹ By faith the people passed through the Red Sea as on dry land; but when the Egyptians tried to do so, they were drowned.

³⁰ By faith the walls of Jericho fell, after the people had marched around them for seven days.

³¹ By faith the prostitute Rahab, because she welcomed the spies, was not killed with those who were disobedient.

³² And what more shall I say? I do not have time to tell about
Gideon, Barak, Samson, Jephthah, David, Samuel and the prophets, ³³ who through faith conquered kingdoms, administered justice, and gained what was promised; who shut the mouths of lions, ³⁴ quenched the fury of the flames, and escaped the edge of the

sword; whose weakness was turned to strength; and who became powerful in battle and routed foreign armies. [35] Women received back their dead, raised to life again. Others were tortured and refused to be released, so that they might gain a better resurrection.[36] Some faced jeers and flogging, while still others were chained and put in prison. [37] They were stoned; they were sawed in two; they were put to death by the sword. They went about in sheepskins and goatskins, destitute, persecuted and mistreated— [38] the world was not worthy of them. They wandered in deserts and mountains, and in caves and holes in the ground.

[39] These were all commended for their faith, yet none of them received what had been promised. [40] God had planned something better for us so that only together with us would they be made perfect.

THE ROMANS ROAD OF SALVATION

Everyone needs salvation because we have all sinned.

Romans 3:10-12, and 23
As it is written, There is no one righteous, not even one;

The penalty, price and consequence of sin is death.

Romans 6:23
For the wages of sin is death, but the gift of God is eternal life in Christ Jesus our Lord

Jesus Christ died for our sins. He paid the price for our sins, he took the punishment for us, and he paid the price for the sins of the world on the cross.

Romans 5:8
But God demonstrates his own love for us in

this: While we were still sinners, Christ died for us.

We receive salvation and eternal life through faith in Jesus Christ.

Romans 10:9-10, and 13
If you declare with your mouth, "Jesus is Lord," and believe in your heart that God raised him from the dead, you will be saved. For it is with your heart that you believe and are justified, and it is with your mouth that you profess your faith and are saved. For, "Everyone who calls on the name of the Lord will be saved. Salvation through Jesus Christ brings us into a relationship of peace with God.

Romans 5:1
Therefore, since we have been justified through faith, we have peace with God through our Lord Jesus Christ,

Romans 8:1
Therefore, there is now no condemnation for those who are in Christ Jesus,

Roman 8:38-39
And I am convinced that nothing can ever separate us from God's love. Neither death nor life

Responding to Romans Road

The Romans Road leads to the path of truth, you can receive God's free gift of salvation today. The following is the way to walk the path down the Romans Road:

Admit you are a sinner and in need of a Savior.

Realize that the penalty for sin is death which leads to eternal separation from God.

Believe Jesus Christ died on the cross to pay the penalty for your sin to save you from sin and death. By the power of Christ's shed blood you have been redeemed.

Repent by turning from your old life of sin to a new life in Jesus Christ. Ask God to forgive you of your sins.

Receive, through faith in Jesus Christ, his free gift of salvation. Ask the Lord Jesus Christ, into your heart and into your life.

ABOUT THE AUTHOR

Mary Annthipie Bane is a wife and mother of three sons, a former homeschooler and an early childhood educator.

Mary has over fifteen years of Christian service and ministry experience. She holds a Bachelor of Biblical Studies from Ames Christian University and a Master of Christian Education from Andersonville Theological Seminary.

Look for these titles coming soon
"Raised in His Ways"
The Value of Christian Values

and the following Christian Fiction titles

"To Have and to Hold"
"A Life To Belong To"
"A Wolf in the Sheepfold"
"The Ornament Box"